Destiny And The Bully

Uquay Baker

Archway Publishing books may be ordered through booksellers or by contacting:

Archway Publishing
1663 Liberty Drive
Bloomington, IN 47403
www.archwaypublishing.com
844-669-3957

Because of the dynamic nature of the Internet, any web addresses or links contained in this book may have changed since publication and may no longer be valid. The views expressed in this work are solely those of the author and do not necessarily reflect the views of the publisher, and the publisher hereby disclaims any responsibility for them.

Any people depicted in stock imagery provided by Getty Images are models, and such images are being used for illustrative purposes only.
Certain stock imagery © Getty Images.

ISBN: 978-1-6657-3308-3 (sc)
ISBN: 978-1-6657-3307-6 (e)

Print information available on the last page.

Archway Publishing rev. date: 11/11/2022

Destiny and the Bully

My name is Destiny
And I will tell you how I became free
From a girl named Karen who was a bully

I come from a small family
It was just my mom and me
And she taught me with hard work, I can be anything I want to be

I love going to school
I even have a classmate from Istanbul
My science teacher taught me about molecules

Then a new student came to our class
And at recess she pushed me in the grass
When the bell rang, she stood in the door and wouldn't let me pass

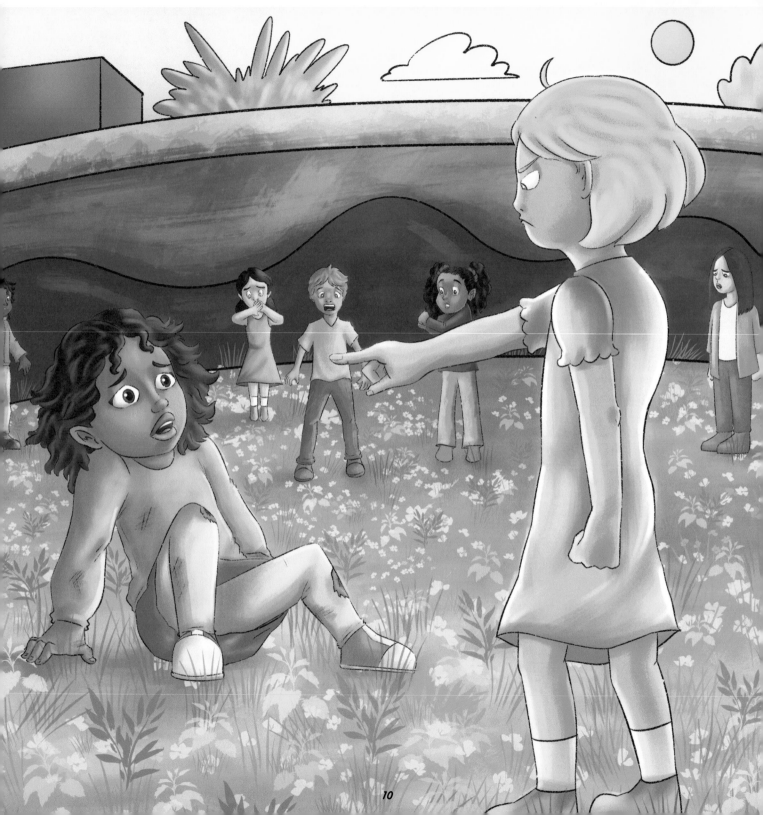

My knee was bleeding, and I was in pain
My pants got dirty and had a nasty stain
Everyone was looking at me and I felt ashamed

But I did not understand
How being mean was part of her plan
She began to make a lot of demands

Karen told me to bring her food
And she ate mine's too-how rude!
I need to do something, or I am screwed

My friends were scared of her too
Everyone in the school already knew
I felt hopeless and didn't know what to do

Maybe I should just run and hide
Never let her catch me inside
And gain back some of my pride

But she always sat with me on the bus
She was loud, rude, and always made a fuss
No one ever wanted to sit near us

I even thought about playing sick
Yes, that might do the trick!
Or maybe even hitting her with a stick?

But that's not very bright
And I know that it's not right
Plus, I don't know how to fight

All I could think of was trying to bail
So, I went home and told my mom the tale
She spoke very calmly and did not yell

Let me tell you a story about people who are mean
Their lives are often so sad they want to scream
You don't know what's going on behind the scenes

They see someone they wish they could be like
They don't know how to express it, just know how to fight
They're mad at the world and want to strike

Bullies don't pick on everyone
They have no friends and don't know how to have fun
When the shoe is on the other foot, they run

I promise you these words are harsh but true
I can't fight this battle for you
It is something you are going to have to do

Destiny didn't sleep much that night
But she knew in her heart her mom was right
She must face her fears with all her might

When Karen got on the bus, Destiny stood on her feet
"You cannot sit in this seat
And I didn't bring you anything to eat!"

All the students stopped talking and the bus got quiet
Who knows what will happen next? A riot?
Karen saw the look on Destiny's face and decided not to try it!

The students clapped and began to cheer
See Destiny didn't know all the students were also in fear
And in that moment, Destiny became hero of the year!

Printed in the United States
by Baker & Taylor Publisher Services